Sharks

with Angel Finn, shark expert

Stephen Savage

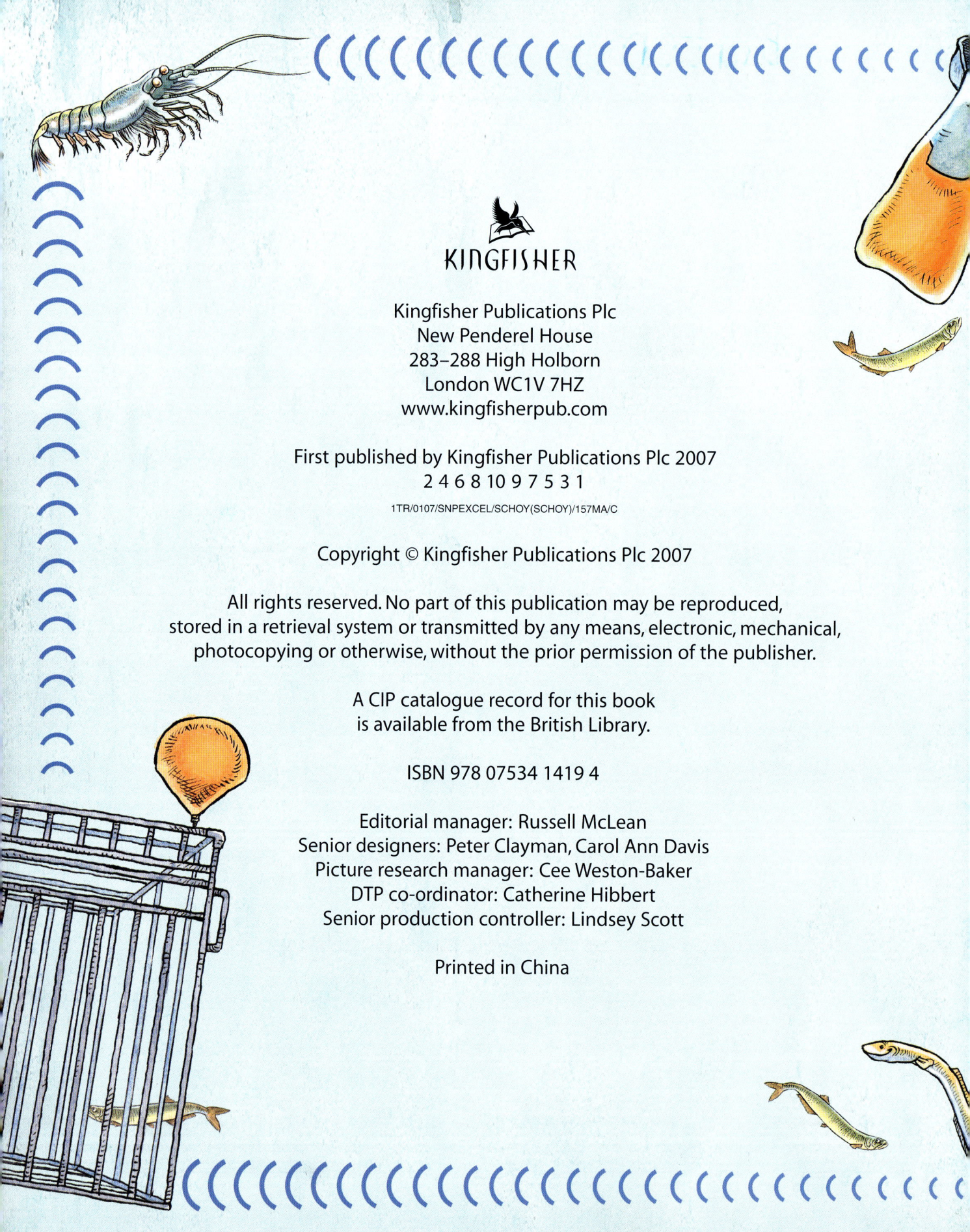

KINGFISHER

Kingfisher Publications Plc
New Penderel House
283–288 High Holborn
London WC1V 7HZ
www.kingfisherpub.com

First published by Kingfisher Publications Plc 2007
2 4 6 8 10 9 7 5 3 1

1TR/0107/SNPEXCEL/SCHOY(SCHOY)/157MA/C

A CIP catalogue record for this book
is available from the British Library.

ISBN 978 07534 1419 4

Editorial manager: Russell McLean
Senior designers: Peter Clayman, Carol Ann Davis
Picture research manager: Cee Weston-Baker
DTP co-ordinator: Catherine Hibbert
Senior production controller: Lindsey Scott

Printed in China

Contents

Meet your guide

Hello, my name is Angel Finn. I am a marine biologist and I study sharks. Sharks are fish, and they live in almost every sea and ocean. Here at the Shark Centre we study sharks close up. They have a large tail for swimming, a dorsal fin to keep them upright and pectoral fins for steering. A shark's bones are made of bendy cartilage.

dorsal fin

black-tipped reef shark

pectoral fin

A shark's skin is covered in tiny skin teeth called dermal denticles. These protect the shark from other animals and help it to swim quickly and quietly.

great white shark skin

"Shark skin is very rough. My leg has a scar where a shark brushed past me."

swimming sharks

People think all sharks are dangerous, but that's not true. In fact, sharks have more to fear from humans, but I will tell you about that later. I love watching sharks swim. The great white is one of the fastest. Like all big sharks, it has to keep swimming or it will sink and drown.

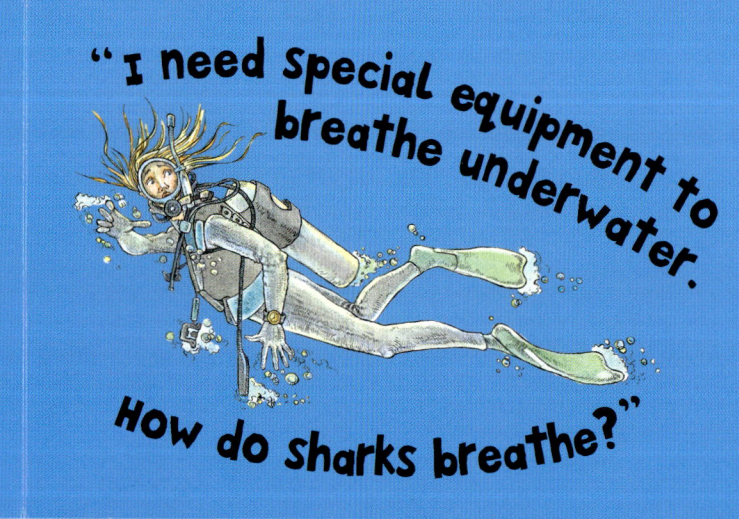

"I need special equipment to breathe underwater.

How do sharks breathe?"

Spiracle

epaulette shark

Small sharks, such as this epaulette shark, can rest on the seabed. They pump water and oxygen to their gills through a hole called a spiracle, so they can breathe even when they are not swimming.

great white shark

Ancient sharks

Sharks have lived in the oceans since before the time of the dinosaurs. Many of a shark's features have not changed since then, but some ancient sharks looked very strange. The dorsal fin of stethacanthus had a flat top covered in rough dermal denticles.

dorsal fin

stethacanthus

megalodon shark

The prehistoric megalodon shark looked like a great white shark, but twice as long. It had few enemies and its favourite food was whales.

prehistoric whale

"Megalodon had really big teeth. This fossilized tooth is larger than my hand."

warm waters

To study sharks, you have to get in the water with them. I have swum with sharks all over the world – sand tiger sharks and white sharks off Australia, blue sharks in the Atlantic Ocean and basking sharks in the warm waters around the British Isles.

sand tiger shark

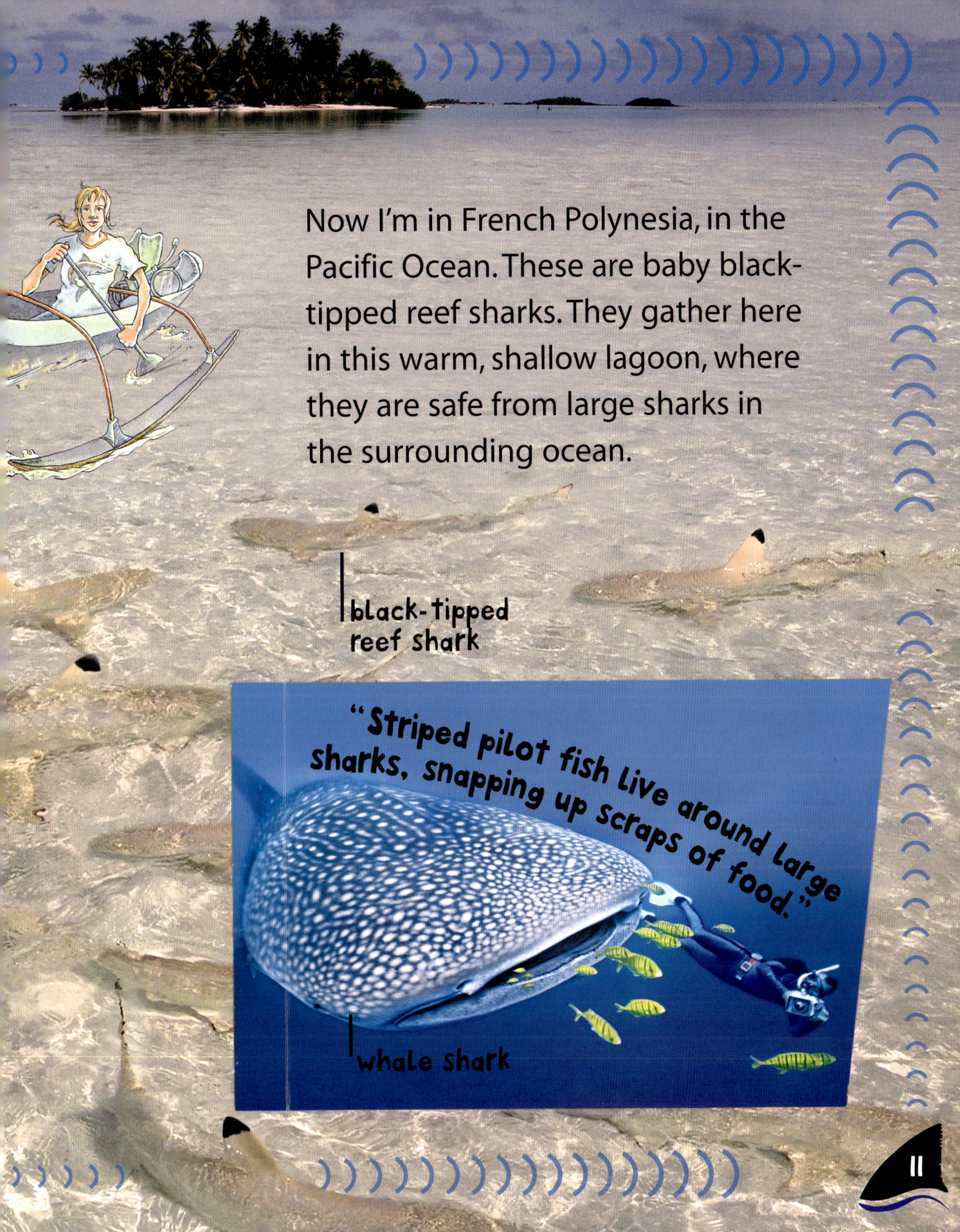

Now I'm in French Polynesia, in the Pacific Ocean. These are baby black-tipped reef sharks. They gather here in this warm, shallow lagoon, where they are safe from large sharks in the surrounding ocean.

black-tipped reef shark

"Striped pilot fish live around large sharks, snapping up scraps of food."

whale shark

Deep waters

A few sharks, such as this large Greenland shark, live in icy polar waters. They swim slowly because of the cold. We know very little about sharks that live in deep water. The megamouth shark was discovered in 1976, and has only been seen about ten times.

Lantern shark

megamouth shark

Greenland shark

I use a submersible to see sharks that live in deep water. Lantern sharks glow in the dark. Males have a different pattern of lights to the females, so they can find each other in the gloom.

"At 1,000 metres deep the water pressure would squash me flat, but this Greenland shark is happy here!"

size, shape and colour

Look at the size of that whale shark! It's the biggest fish in the sea, but is completely harmless to people. Whale sharks eat plankton and small fish, which they filter from huge mouthfuls of seawater. A few sharks, such as this tiny pygmy shark, are very small indeed.

"This pygmy shark is the smallest type of shark."

pygmy shark

horn shark

Most sharks are grey and white, so they blend in with the sea. But small sharks, such as the horn shark, can be sandy coloured, spotted or striped. This helps them to hide on the seabed, safe from larger predators.

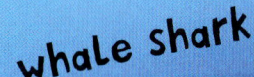

whale shark

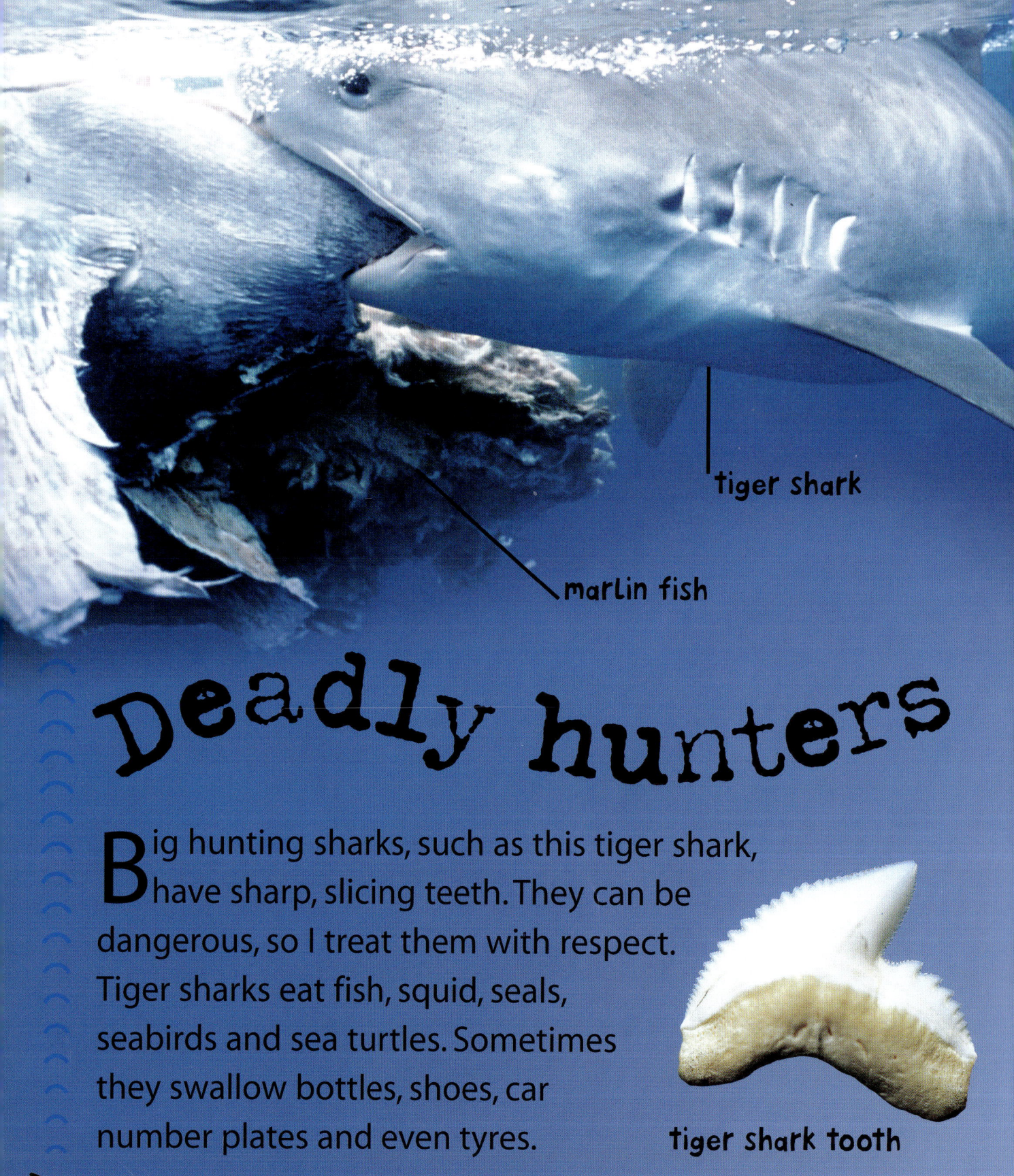

tiger shark

marlin fish

Deadly hunters

Big hunting sharks, such as this tiger shark, have sharp, slicing teeth. They can be dangerous, so I treat them with respect. Tiger sharks eat fish, squid, seals, seabirds and sea turtles. Sometimes they swallow bottles, shoes, car number plates and even tyres.

tiger shark tooth

What happens if a shark loses one of its teeth?

Copper sharks often follow huge shoals of sardines. There are thousands of fish in each shoal. The sharks swim through the shoal, gulping down mouthfuls of the sardines.

copper shark

Sardines _____

catching food

Not all sharks feed on large animals. Sharks that live on the ocean floor often use camouflage to help them catch small prey. This Australian wobbegong shark looks like the seabed. It ambushes crabs and fish that swim by. Cookiecutter sharks bite small, round chunks of flesh from dolphins and fish.

cookiecutter shark

This large basking shark filters tiny fish and plankton out of the water. It has bristly gill rakers that sieve the food from huge mouthfuls of seawater.

basking shark

"The flaps of skin around a wobbegong's mouth look just like pieces of seaweed."

wobbegong shark

skin flap

Why do sharks bite metal cages?

shark senses

Sharks find food, avoid danger and look for a mate using their amazing senses. Did you know that a shark's sense of smell is 10,000 times better than yours or mine? It can smell the tiniest amounts of blood from an injured fish. The hammerhead shark has a hammer-shaped head which may help its senses to work even better.

injured fish

Sharks have good hearing and can even feel other animals moving. They see best in the dim light at dawn and dusk. Some smaller sharks have barbels, which they use to feel for prey hidden in the sand.

barbel

nurse shark

hammerhead shark

vibration from fish

studying sharks

I'm in Africa helping with a study of endangered great white sharks. I am taking photographs of this shark's dorsal fin. Every shark's fin has different marks and patterns. These allow us to give the shark a number and recognize it if it swims past again.

shark SA087   shark SA209

"South Africa has the biggest population of great white sharks."

tag

This scientist is putting a tag on a shark's fin. The tag collects information on where the shark travels and how deep it dives. One shark, called Nicole, swam from Africa to Australia and back. That's a trip of about 20,000 kilometres!

tag

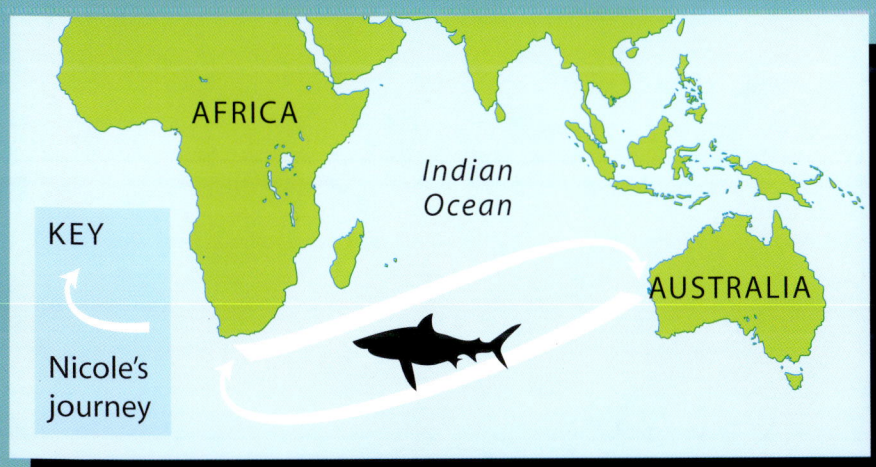

AFRICA

Indian Ocean

AUSTRALIA

KEY

Nicole's journey

ocean predators

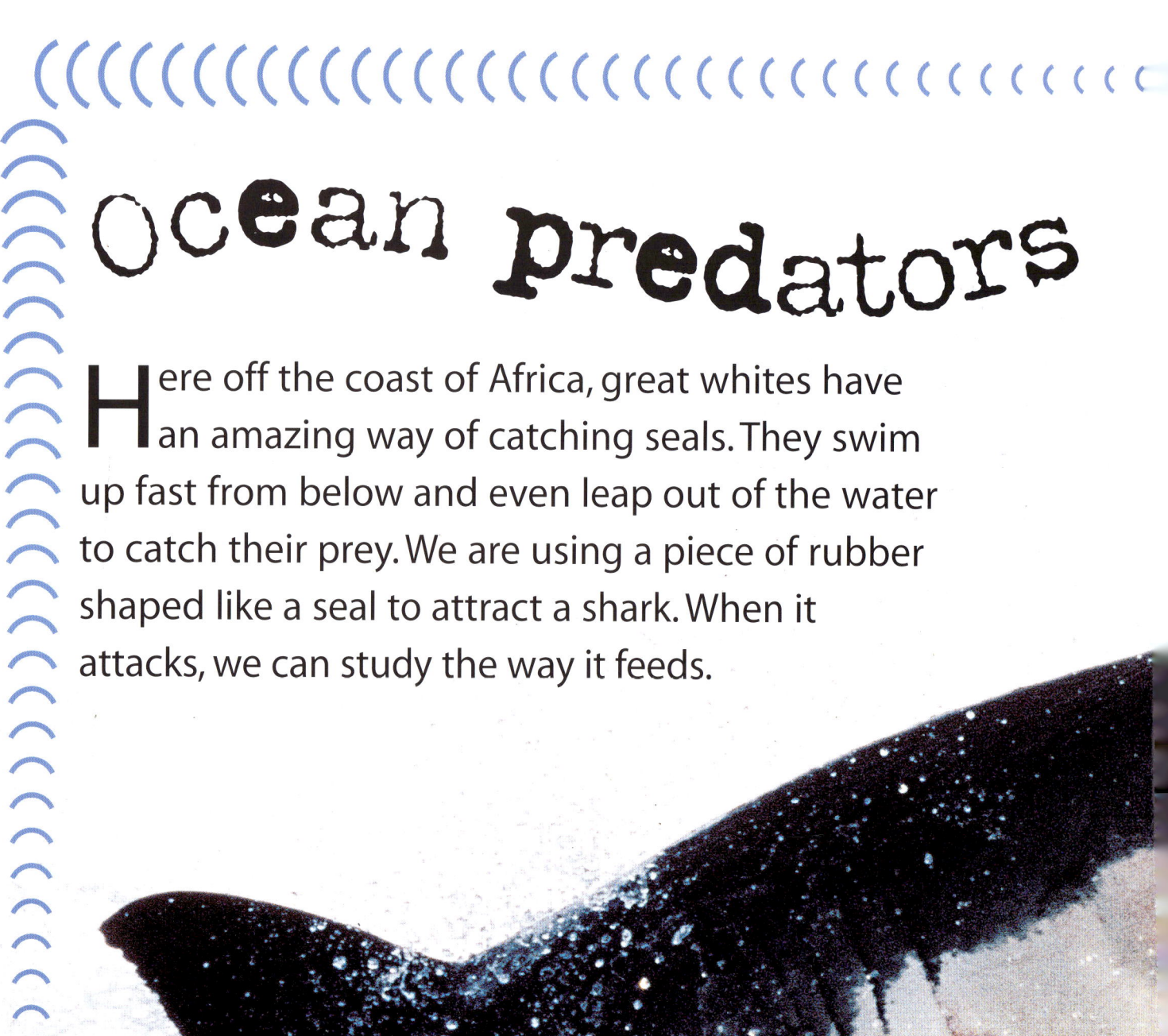

Here off the coast of Africa, great whites have an amazing way of catching seals. They swim up fast from below and even leap out of the water to catch their prey. We are using a piece of rubber shaped like a seal to attract a shark. When it attacks, we can study the way it feeds.

It may seem sad that sharks eat seals, but this helps to keep the ocean food chain in balance. If the number of seals is too high, they will eat too many fish.

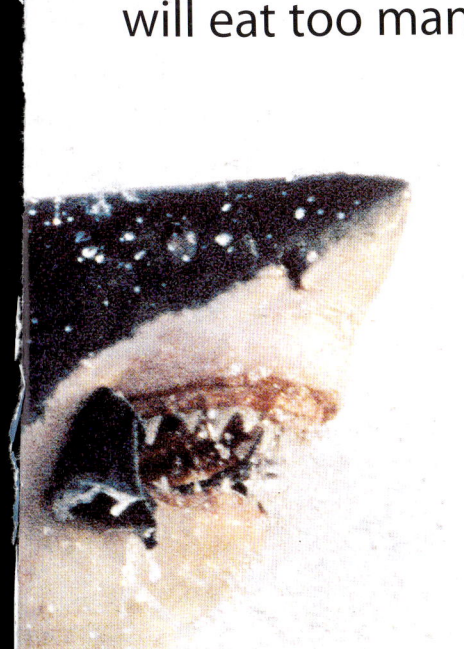

Great whites eat seals, but what do seals eat?

"Sharks help to keep the oceans healthy by eating sick and dying animals."

shark babies

All sharks produce eggs, but many female sharks keep their eggs inside their body. The young sharks hatch and the mother gives birth. Some small types of shark lay special egg cases. The baby shark grows inside until it is ready to hatch. A baby shark is called a pup.

horn shark egg case

adult lemon shark

newborn
lemon shark

Sharks only lay a few eggs, because they are big and can take several months to hatch. Here at the Shark Centre we often have shark eggs developing. When they hatch, we return the baby sharks to the sea.

which shark grows in this egg case?

"Sharks often give birth in shallow water, where they are safer from ocean predators."

sharks in danger

Looking at these powerful but beautiful blue sharks, it's hard to believe that many sharks are now endangered. Hundreds of thousands of sharks are killed each year. Some are caught for food, while others are killed to make souvenirs from their jaws.

copper shark caught in a net

"Each year, more people are killed by falling coconuts than by sharks!"

blue shark

Sharks are not the dangerous killers that many of us think them to be. I hope my work will help you understand sharks better, and that you will tell other people how amazing sharks really are.

Glossary

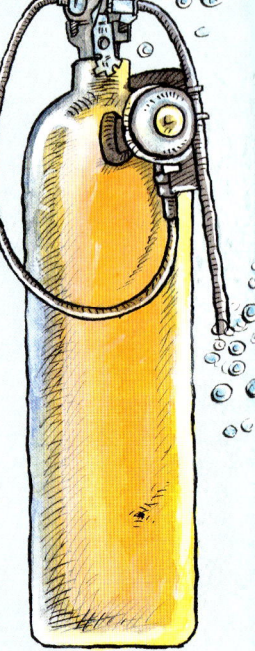

barbels Feelers beneath some sharks' mouths that help them to touch and taste.

camouflage A shape, colour or pattern that helps an animal to blend in with its surroundings.

cartilage A light, bendy material that makes up a shark's skeleton. Your ear flaps are made of cartilage.

dermal denticles Small, tooth-like scales that cover a shark's skin.

embryo A baby animal in an early stage of development.

endangered In danger of dying out.

filter To separate out food, such as plankton, from water.

food chain The links between different animals that feed on plants and each other.

gill The part of a fish's body that takes oxygen from water so that the fish can breathe.

gill raker A comb-like part of the gills of some sharks. It is used to filter food.

oxygen A gas in air and in water. All animals need oxygen to live.

plankton Tiny animals and plants that live in the sea.

predator An animal that hunts and eats another animal.

prey Animals eaten by other animals.

shellfish A sea creature with a hard shell, such as a crab or a lobster.

shoal A large number of fish swimming together.

water pressure The weight of water in the ocean.

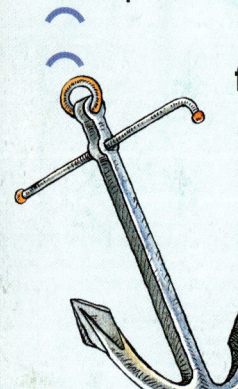

Index

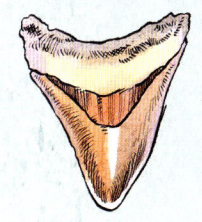

Acknowledgements

The publisher would like to thank the following for permission to reproduce their material. Every care has been taken to trace copyright holders. However, if there have been unintentional omissions or failure to trace copyright holders, we apologize and will, if informed, endeavour to make corrections in any future edition.

Key: *b* = bottom, *c* = centre, *l* = left, *r* = right, *t* = top

Cover: Nature Picture Library/Brandon Cole; pages 4–5 Oceanwide Images/Gary Bell; 5 Corbis/Clouds Hill Imaging; 6–7 Corbis/Denis Scott; 7 Oceanwide Images/Gary Bell; 10 Nature Picture Library/Jeff Rotman; 10–11 Ardea/Valerie Taylor; 11 SeaPics/James Watt; 12*bl* SeaPics/Tom Haight; 12*cr* SeaPics/Espen Rekdal; 13 SeaPics/Saul Gonor; 14–15 Corbis/Loule Psihoyos; 14*bl* Imagequest Marine/Masa Ushioda; 15*tl* Oxford Scientific Films; 16*t* SeaPics/Ben Cropp Productions; 16*br* SeaPics/Franco Banfi; 17 SeaPics/Doug Perrine; 18 C. Bento/Australian Museum; 19*t* SeaPics/Saul Gonor; 19*b* SeaPics/Gary Bell; 20*tl* Photolibrary/Carl Roessler; 20*br* Getty Images/Johner; 20–21 Nature Picture Library/Doug Perrine; 21*tr* Imagequest Marine/Masa Ushioda; 22*tc* SeaPics/Doug Perrine; 22*tr* Nature Picture Library/Mark Carwadine; 22*b* Nature Picture Library/Jurgen Freund; 23*t* Alamy/Eric Nathan; 23*b* Nature Picture Library/Jeff Rotman; 24–25 SeaPics/C&M Fallows; 26–27 Nature Picture Library/Doug Perrine; 26*tr* SeaPics/Howard Hall; 28–29 SeaPics/Michael S. Nolan; 28*tl* SeaPics/Vance Wiese

The publisher would like to thank the following illustrators:
Sebastian Quigley 4–5, 8–9, 18–19, 22–23;
Lyn Stone (Angel Finn and incidentals throughout);
Peter Winfield 6, 14, 17, 23, 25, 27

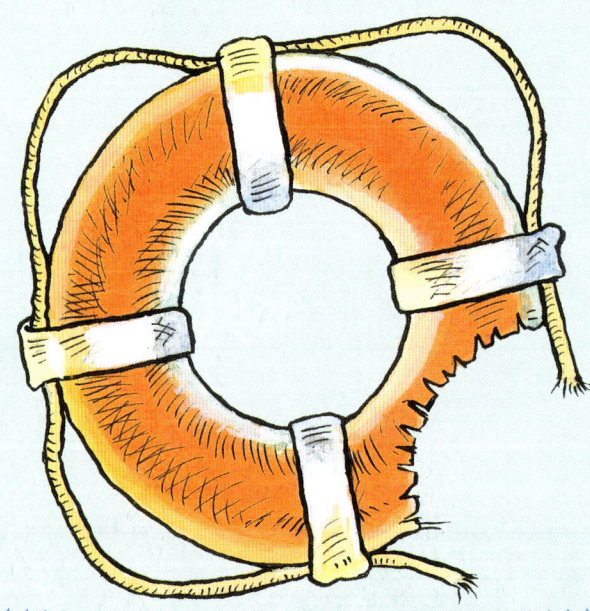